Babe Ruth

HOME RUN HERO

Babe Ruth

HOME RUN HERO

by Keith Brandt
illustrated by Hal Frenck

Troll Associates

Library of Congress Cataloging in Publication Data

Brandt, Keith, (date)
    Babe Ruth, home run hero.

    Summary: A brief biography of the first great home
run hitter in baseball history.
    1. Ruth, Babe, 1895-1945—Juvenile literature.
2. Baseball players—United States—Biography—Juvenile
literature. [1. Ruth, Babe, 1895-1945. 2. Baseball
players] I. Frenck, Hal, ill. II. Title.
GV865.R8B73   1986   796.357′092′4 [B] [92]   85-1091
ISBN 0-8167-0553-4 (lib. bdg.)
ISBN 0-8167-0554-2 (pbk.)

Babe Ruth

HOME RUN HERO

It was game number three of the 1932 baseball World Series. The date was October 1, and
the New York Yankees were playing against the
Chicago Cubs. It was the fifth inning, and the
score was tied, 4–4. One of baseball's most
dramatic moments was about to take place.

The great Yankee player, Babe Ruth, was at bat. The Chicago pitcher, Charlie Root, was being very careful with every pitch he threw. He didn't want the top home-run hitter in the major leagues to blast the ball out of the stadium.

Ruth was just as determined to get a hit. He always enjoyed hitting and playing baseball. But today was special. Ruth was angry at the Chicago fans, who were booing and throwing things at him from the stands. He was angry at the Chicago players, who had been yelling insults at him since the start of the World Series.

Now the crowd was roaring for Root to strike out the Yankee slugger. The count was two balls and two strikes. One more strike and Ruth would be out. The players were screaming at him from the Cubs' bench. He glared at them, then turned and faced the pitcher. Suddenly, Ruth smiled and pointed toward the distant

center-field fence. He seemed to be saying,
"Throw me your best pitch. I'm going to hit it
over that fence!"

On the next pitch, the Yankee star swung, the bat connected, and the ball flew high over the center-field fence. It was right where he had pointed! Ruth couldn't have placed the ball better if he had carried it there in his hands. It was also the longest hit in the history of Chicago's Wrigley Field. With that dramatic home run to inspire them, the Yankees went on to win the game, and the 1932 World Series.

George Herman Ruth, one of the greatest baseball players of all time, was born on February 6, 1895, in Baltimore, Maryland. He didn't get the nickname "Babe" until he began his professional baseball career. Before then, he was called George, or Little George, because his father was also named George.

Mr. and Mrs. Ruth were poor, uneducated people. Because they never had much money, they were forced to move from one apartment to another in a run-down Baltimore neighborhood. Mr. Ruth worked as a lightning-rod salesman, a wagon driver (in the days before there were automobiles), a laborer, a saloonkeeper, and a harness salesman. No job ever lasted very long.

Kate Schamberger Ruth, Little George's mother, was in poor health most of the time. Her life was harsh and often sad. Although she gave birth to eight children, only two lived past childhood. These were George and his younger sister, Mamie.

Mrs. Ruth tried to give the family a decent home. But the problems of her life were too many. Mrs. Ruth was simply unable to take good care of Little George.

As soon as the young boy could walk, he was out roaming the streets. On many days he went without a solid meal. Sometimes the small boy, not yet old enough to go to school, put together his own dinner from what little food was in the apartment. Baths and clean clothes were as rare in George's life as a decent meal. He survived those early years almost like a stray animal, alone and unwanted.

George's only real love and attention came from his mother's parents. The Schambergers fed their grandson when he came to visit, and gave him the affection he didn't get at home. Mr. and Mrs. Schamberger were German immigrants who spoke only German. Little George picked up their language quickly. In fact, he spoke German before he spoke English. Most of the English that he learned before he was school age was what he heard in the streets.

Mr. and Mrs. Ruth were not good parents. Most of the time they paid no attention to George at all. Between them, the Ruths made their son feel worthless and unloved. It was a childhood that a writer would later describe as "no childhood at all." Ruth agreed with this. He said, "I had a rotten start, and it took me a long time to get my bearings."

When George reached school age, his life remained the same. His parents said nothing when he didn't bother to go to school. Day after day, he roamed the streets with other aimless boys. They taught him to swear, to chew tobacco, to steal apples from fruit stands, and to fight.

"I was a bum when I was a kid," Ruth said sadly, recalling those early years. "Looking back on my boyhood, I honestly don't remember being aware of the difference between right and wrong."

When George was six years old, his parents bought a saloon. George spent a lot of time there, even though it was a terrible place for a young boy to be. Then, late in the spring of 1902, there was a big fight in the saloon. Shots were fired, and the police were called. One of the officers learned that a small child was there when the shooting took place. Not only that, a

neighbor told the officer, the boy was there at
all hours of the day, and never went to school.
The police reported this, and the proper
authorities took action.

On June 13, 1902, Mr. Ruth and George took a trolley-car ride across the city of Baltimore. They got off at St. Mary's Industrial School for Boys. The court had ordered the Ruths to place their son in the school for his own well-being. George was only seven-and-a-half years old. The order said that he would have to stay at the school until his twenty-first birthday.

St. Mary's Industrial School for Boys was made up of six large, gray buildings. Each stood three stories high. There was a broad playing field on the grounds, but it was little more than a bare, dusty area. Eight hundred boys were housed and cared for at the school. Some, like George, were sent there because they had been neglected at home. Some were orphans in need of shelter. Still others were runaways or boys who had gotten into trouble with the law. There were no real criminals at St. Mary's, just youngsters who needed care and guidance.

At first, George was homesick and unhappy. He cried all the time. He hated having to wear the denim overalls that were the school uniform. The dormitory where he slept had two hundred beds, and George found it a scary place to be. He missed his little sister, his grandparents, and his friends.

St. Mary's was run by Catholic brothers. But the school took in boys of all faiths. The only requirement was that the child need their help. The brothers were teachers, coaches, cooks, carpenters, painters, and craftsmen. They were there to teach any boy who was willing to learn. The brothers were friends and advisors who believed their main job was to turn out honorable, decent young men.

It took George a while to get used to the routine at St. Mary's. The boys went to bed at eight o'clock every night and got up at six every morning. After washing and dressing, they went to chapel. Chapel was followed by a breakfast of oatmeal, bread and butter, and a glass of milk. Classes started at seven-thirty and continued until lunch hour. Lunch was the main meal of the day. It was always hot, fresh, and filling.

The cooking wasn't fancy at the school. But it was nutritious, and the boys always had enough to eat. This was a change for some of them, including George, who had never been sure of when or where he would eat his next meal.

St. Mary's had boys as young as five and as old as twenty-one. Until they reached the age of fourteen, the youngsters attended morning and afternoon classes. The older boys had only three hours of class time a day. Their afternoons were spent learning a trade, to prepare themselves for life as adults.

For boys of all ages, the late afternoons and all day Sunday were set aside for sports. The sports included football, soccer, handball, basketball, volleyball, foot races, boxing, wrestling, and ice skating. But the most important sport at St. Mary's was baseball. There were forty-three teams at the school. Each one had a name, uniforms, and a regular playing schedule.

The brothers were just as enthusiastic about baseball as the boys. They were fans themselves, who enjoyed coaching and watching a good game. Even so, baseball and the rest of the sports program had another, more important purpose than just fun and exercise.

Most of the boys, like George, hadn't been part of a team before. They didn't know how to play together, to help others, or to settle arguments except by fighting. The brothers used sports to teach self-discipline, honesty, fairness, team play, and how to win and lose.

As George settled into the daily routine, he found that St. Mary's wasn't such a bad place at all. For the first time in his life, George Herman Ruth was clean, well fed, and warmly dressed.

George never liked classwork, but at St. Mary's he did learn to read and write. When he first arrived, he could not read a single number or letter. He barely spoke a complete English sentence. He was laughed at by the other boys because he had to attend classes with younger children. This made him feel stupid and unable to learn. This was a feeling that stayed with him all his life.

The afternoon sports didn't end until the supper bell rang. Then, after eating, the boys had band or choir practice, and time to go to the canteen. The canteen was a small building on the school grounds. It sold candy, cakes, peanuts, and other snacks. The boys did not have money to spend. Instead, they paid for snacks with credits earned by work they did around the school.

George liked candy and cake, and any other kind of sweet. Before he came to St. Mary's, these were rare treats for him, and now it seemed he could never get enough. Still, he always shared his snacks with friends. This generosity stayed part of Babe Ruth's character even when he was an adult. As a baseball star he earned a great deal of money, and he spent it freely on his friends.

George's huge appetite for food also stayed with him. Part of the Babe Ruth legend is the number of hot dogs he ate before, during, and after ball games; the gallons of ice cream he enjoyed in one sitting; and his meals that could have filled the stomachs of three normal eaters.

As much as young George liked food, there was something he liked even more. He loved playing baseball. The baseball field was the only place where he was a success.

31

George struggled with reading and arithmetic. He was so homely that the other boys made fun of his face, and they laughed at the way he walked with his toes pointing inward. He was clumsy and forgetful. He still felt lonely and unloved. But at baseball he was a natural. He could hit better than any other boy his age. He could throw and run and catch as if he had done nothing else since the day he was born.

George played the game twelve months a year. When it wasn't baseball season, some boys still used the bat and ball. If there weren't enough players for a regular game, they had a two-player game they called "pokenins." One player was the batter. He stood in front of a wall, facing the pitcher. The batter kept hitting until the pitcher got him out. Then the boys changed places. When George Ruth pitched, he put out the other boy fast. When George was batting, he hit one pitch after another.

George's baseball abilities caught the attention of Brother Matthias, who was in charge of sports at the school. Brother Matthias stood over six feet tall and was a powerful man.

He didn't have to yell or raise his voice to be obeyed. The boys respected him because he was as fair as he was tough.

For George, Brother Matthias was more than just a teacher. He was a combination of father, friend, coach, and advisor. He realized that George could be helped through baseball. The sport could be used to give him a future. It could also be used to teach the boy discipline, pride in himself, and to win the admiration of the other boys. With all this in mind, Brother Matthias began to concentrate on getting George to make the most of his gifts.

They spent hours together on the ball field, practicing every part of the game. Many years later, Babe Ruth said, "I always felt I could hit the ball, even the first time I held a bat. But Brother Matthias taught some other things. He made me a pitcher and showed me how to field. He really knew the game of baseball and he loved it." Ruth also described Brother Matthias as the greatest man he had ever known.

As George entered his teen years, his out-standing play won many games for St. Mary's and brought him the respect of the other boys. He still might have classes with young children, but it was a different story on the baseball diamond. There, he was placed with the oldest players at the school—and he was better than any of them.

When George reached his fourteenth birth-day, he began to learn the shirt-making trade. His part of the job was putting collars on shirts, for which he earned a canteen credit of six cents for each shirt. George enjoyed the work, and became quite good at it. Even when he was the highest paid baseball player in America, he took pleasure in removing a worn collar from one of his expensive silk shirts and replacing it with a new collar. He didn't do it to save the cost of a new shirt. The world's greatest baseball player simply was proud of the skill that had never left him.

By the age of sixteen, George was almost six feet tall. Pictures of him as an adult show him as a heavy man. But as a boy he was thin. It was only when he grew older that he gained weight, reaching 215 pounds during the peak years of his career. Yet Babe Ruth's arms and legs remained slim. He never looked too muscular, but even as a youngster he was exceptionally strong.

Sixteen-year-old George played for one of the best teams at St. Mary's. The school's top teams were part of a league with other schools in the Baltimore area. Each team was named after a major-league baseball club. George played for the Red Sox. In 1912, when his team won the school championship, he was its catcher. At this time, however, Brother Matthias began developing the left-handed youngster into a pitcher. It wasn't long before Ruth was the finest pitcher St. Mary's had ever seen.

George's hitting was also extraordinary. Time and again he drove the ball more than four hundred feet from home plate, which is more than most professional ballplayers can do. The teenager also hit over sixty home runs in one of his seasons with the St. Mary's Red Sox.

That number would become significant during Ruth's professional career. In the 1927 season, he hit sixty home runs. It was a record that stood until Roger Maris, of the New York Yankees, hit sixty-one home runs in 1961. (Roger Maris had an important advantage. The 1961 season had 162 games, while the 1927 season had only 154 games.)

George Ruth was soon recognized as the best pitcher and hitter in the Baltimore high-school league. By 1913, when he was eighteen, his brilliance as a baseball player came to the attention of Jack Dunn. Mr. Dunn was the owner of the Baltimore Orioles, then a professional minor-league baseball team. Mr. Dunn watched the tall, strong teen-ager pitch one game. That was enough to convince the team owner that the young man had a promising baseball future.

Jack Dunn was ready to give George a contract to pitch for the Orioles. Only one problem stood in their way—Ruth was too

young to sign a legal contract. Then one of the
St. Mary's brothers found a solution. Mr. Dunn
could become George's legal guardian, and sign
the contract for him. Mr. Dunn promised to care
for George as if he were a son, and the papers
were signed. On February 27, 1914, George
Herman Ruth left St. Mary's to join the Orioles
for spring training.

On the ball field, George was an immediate success. Off the field, he wasn't nearly as sure of himself. He was dazzled by a world that was so different from St. Mary's. When George took a ride in an elevator for the first time, he rode up and down in it for hours. When he was given five dollars for expense money, he felt rich. But the biggest thrill of all was learning that he could eat as much food as he wanted, at the team's expense.

George's innocent behavior was funny to the veteran players, who teased him about it constantly. Finally an Oriole coach warned them, "You be careful with the teasing. This boy is one of Mr. Dunn's babes." The teasing stopped, but the nickname "Babe" stuck. From then on, George Herman Ruth always called himself Babe.

That spring saw the birth of one of baseball's greatest careers. During the next twenty-two years, Babe Ruth starred for the Boston Red Sox, New York Yankees, and Boston Braves. In that time, he set pitching and hitting records that lasted for many years. Some still stand unbroken.

The Babe, or the Bambino, as he was affectionately known, was more than baseball's brightest star. He was the symbol of the sport to millions of Americans. Wherever the Babe played, fans packed the stadium.

Babe Ruth finished his long career in the same magical style that had made him an American hero. On May 25, 1935, Babe's team, the Boston Braves, were playing the Pittsburgh Pirates at home, in Forbes Field. The aging slugger was tired and feeling sick. Everyone was saying he was through, that he had lost his ability to play, even to hit.

Babe's pride wouldn't let him go out looking bad. In the first inning of that game, he hit a two-run homer off Pirate pitcher Red Lucas. Two innings later, Ruth hit another two-run homer. This time the pitcher was Guy Bush. In

the fifth inning, against Bush, Ruth hit a single to drive in another run.

In the seventh inning, Babe came to bat again. Bush was still pitching and no runners were on base. He threw the forty-year-old slugger a blazing fastball, and Ruth's bat connected for another home run! It was his third homer of the day, and the 714th of his magnificent career. It was also the kind of home run that had made Ruth a living legend. The ball traveled more than six hundred feet. It sailed over the stadium roof in right field and completely out of the ball park.

As Guy Bush, the Pittsburgh pitcher, later said, "I never saw a ball hit so hard before or since. He was fat and old, but he still had that great swing. Even when he missed, you could hear the bat go swish. I can't remember anything about the first home run he hit off me that day. I guess it was just another homer. But I can't forget that last one. It's probably still going."

Babe Ruth died on August 16, 1948, at the age of fifty-three. He was one of the first players elected to baseball's Hall of Fame. When he died, baseball fans everywhere mourned the passing of a true sports legend.